2

3

O My Soul, My Soul.

By

John C Burt.

Photographs Courtesy of :
   ahmad - odeh.
   juan - chavez.
   bobby - stevenson.
   greg - rakozy.
   vicky - sim.
   aziz - acharki.
Free downloads on :
   unsplash.com

(C) Copyright to John
C Burt 2020. Words
and text.

6

7

8

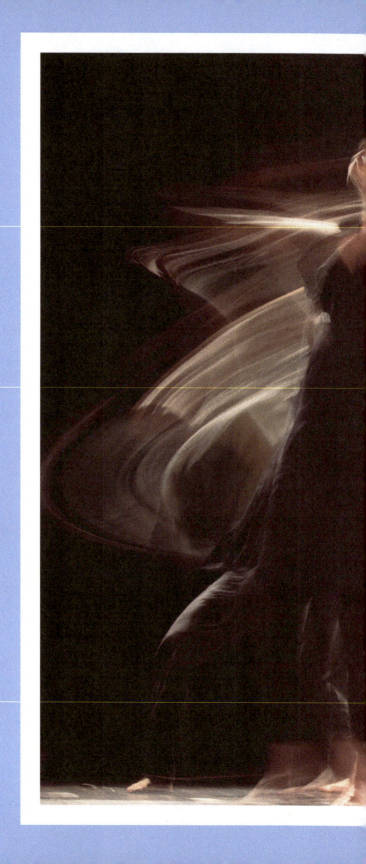

9

10

11

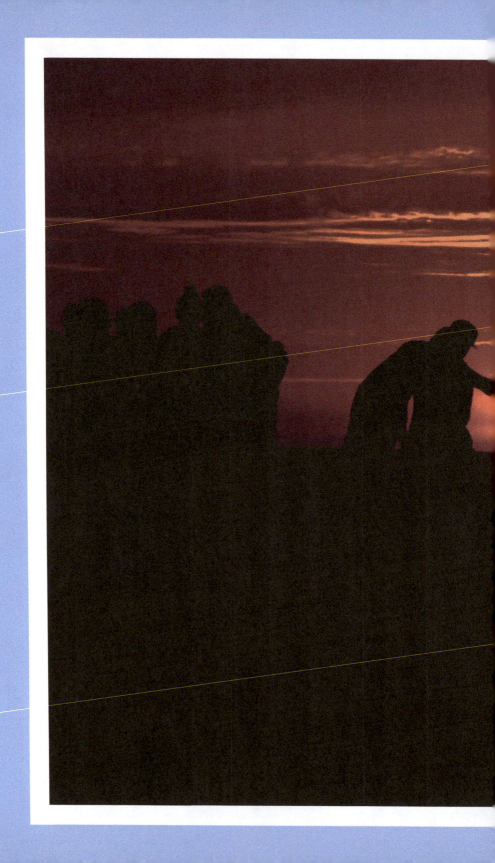

16

17

1.

FOREWORD :

This is a book with the title of ' O My Soul, My Soul ' and it will look at the relationship of our souls to our relationship with the Lord Jesus Christ. As much as King David cried out from the very depths of his own soul, we need to cry out from the depths of our souls to the Lord Jesus Christ. Like him we need to question where our souls are with the Lord Jesus Christ, or as in his case the Lord God Almighty?

One only has to think about many of the Psalms of the Psalter that are attributed to David. They are real and raw cries out from the very depths of the soul of King David, the one who had been a Shepherd Boy? Do we today, cry out from the very depths of our souls like David? I would be of the belief that the Lord Jesus Christ at different times requires this of His follower's in the World - at - large of today. The great thing, is that, he does in fact and reality respond to the cries from the very depths of our souls. At times, not in the way or ways we want Him to but He will in fact respond to us. The Suffering Servant who is the LORD , the Messiah and the coming King will respond to the very cries of our souls from the depths of them !

In the end, the

question which will be the guide and the guidepost's for this book is ' is it well with my soul?' This is the question we always need to be asking of our own souls? ' Is it well with my own soul?' At times, our soul's and our very beings can get so out of whack that it can be like we do not even have a relationship with the Lord Jesus Christ. Yet, the question, remains on the table and needs to be answered by us?

26

27

28

29

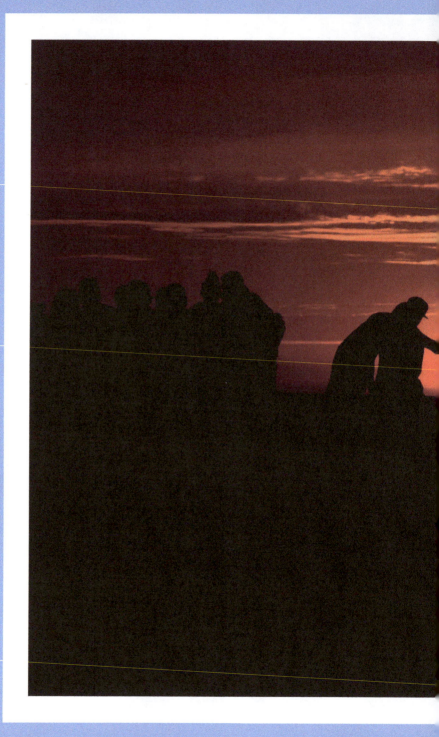

31

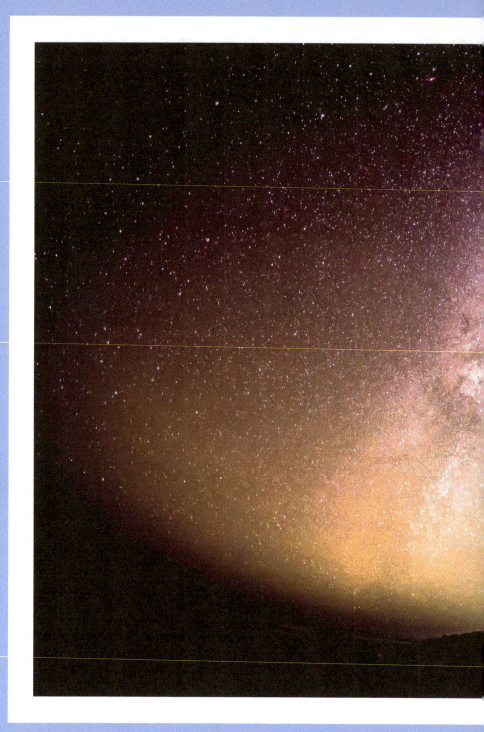

34

35

36

37

2.

Some verses from the Word of God will now be cited. There

will be four different versions of the text's given. They will be the ESV, the NIV, the Voice and the GNT.

(ESV)

Job 7 : 11.
"(11) " Therefore I will not restrain my mouth; I will speak in the anguish of my spirit; I will complain in the bitterness of my soul." "

Job 10 : 1.
"(1) " I loathe my life; I will give free utterance to my complaint; I will speak in the bitterness of my soul." "

Psalm 42 : 5 -6.

"(5) Why are you cast down, O my soul, and why are you in turmoil within me?

Hope in God; for I shall praise him, my salvation (6) and my God.

My soul is cast down within me; therefore I

remember you
    from the land of
Jordan and of
Hermon, from
Mount Mizar."

    Psalm 42 : 11.
    " (11) Why are
you cast down, O my
soul, and why are
you in turmoil
within me?

Hope in God; for I shall again praise him, my salvation and my God."

Psalm 84 : 2.
"(2) My soul longs, yes, faints for the courts of the LORD; my heart and flesh sing for joy to the living GOD."

Psalm 104 : 35.

" (35) Let sinners be consumed from the earth, and let the wicked be no more!

Bless the LORD, O my soul ! Praise the LORD! "

Isaiah 26 : 9.
" (9) My soul
yearns for you in the
night; my spirit
within me earnestly
seeks you.
      For when your
judgments are in
the earth,
      the inhabitants
of the world learn
righteousness."

Isaiah 38 : 15.

" (15) What shall I say? For he has spoken to me,
    and he himself has done it.
    I walk slowly all my years
    because of the bitterness of my soul."

Isaiah 61 : 10.

" (10) I will greatly rejoice in the LORD;
    my soul shall exult in my God,
    for he has clothed me with the garments of salvation;
    he has covered

me with the robe of
righteousness,
 as a bridegroom
decks himself like a
priest with a
beautiful headdress,
 and as a bride
adorns herself with
jewels."

Jeremiah 32 : 41.

"(41) I will rejoice in doing them good, and I will plant them in this land in faithfulness, with all my heart and all my soul."

Micah 6 : 7.

" (7) Will the LORD be pleased with thousands of rams, with ten thousands of rivers of oil?

Shall I give my firstborn for my transgression, the fruit of my body for the sin of my soul?"

Matthew 11 : 29 - 30.

" (29) Take my yoke upon you, and learn from me, for I am gentle and lowly in heart, and you will find rest for your souls.

(30) For my yoke is easy, and my burden is light."

Matthew 26: 37 - 38.

" (37) And taking with him Peter and the two sons of Zebedee, he began to be sorrowful and troubled.

(38) The he said to them," My soul is very sorrowful, even to death; remain here, and watch with me." "

John 12 : 27.

" (27) " Now is my soul troubled. And what shall I say? ' Father, save me from this hour'? But for this purpose I have come to this hour. ' " "

59

3.

(NIV)

Job 7 : 11.
"(11) " Therefore
I will not keep
silent; I will speak

out in the anguish
of my spirit,
    I will complain
in the bitterness of
my soul." "

    Job 10 : 1.
    "(1) " I loathe
my very life;
therefore I will give
free rein to my
complaint and

speak out in the bitterness of my soul." "

Psalm 42 : 5 - 6.
" (5) Why, my soul, are you downcast?
Why so disturbed within me?

Put your hope in God, for I will yet praise him, my Savior and my God.

(6) My soul is downcast within me; therefore I will remember you from the land of the Jordan, the heights of Hermon - from Mount Mizar."

Psalm 42 : 11.

" (11) Why, my soul, are you downcast?

Why so disturbed within me?

Put your hope in God, for I will yet praise him, my Savior and my God. "

Psalm 84 : 2.
" (2) My soul yearns, even faints, for the courts of the LORD; my heart and my flesh cry out for the living God."

Psalm 104 : 35.

" (35) But
may sinners vanish
from the earth
and the
wicked be no more.

Praise the LORD,
my soul.

Praise the LORD."

Isaiah 26 : 9.
" (9) My soul yearns for you in the night; in the morning my spirit longs for you. When your judgments come upon the earth, the people of the world learn righteousness."

Isaiah 38 : 15.
" (15) But
what can I say? He
has spoken to me,
and he himself has
done this.
I will walk
humbly all my
years
because of
this anguish of my

soul."

Isaiah 61 : 10.
" (10) I delight greatly in the LORD; my soul rejoices in my God. For he has clothed me with garments of salvation
and arrayed me

in a robe of his
righteousness,
        as a bridegroom
adorns his head like
a priest.
        and as a bride
adorns herself with
her jewels."

Jeremiah 32 : 41.

"(41) I will rejoice in doing them good and will assuredly plant them in this land with all my heart and soul."

Micah 6 : 7.
"(7) Will the LORD be pleased with thousands of

rams, with ten thousand rivers of olive oil?

Shall I offer my firstborn for my transgression, the fruit of my body for the sin of my soul?"

Matthew 11 : 29 - 30.

"(29)" Take my yoke upon you and learn from me, for I am gentle and humble in heart, and you will find rest for your souls.

(30) For my yoke is easy and my burden is light." "

Matthew 26: 37 - 38.

" (37) He took Peter and the two sons of Zebedee along with him, and he began to be sorrowful and troubled.

(38) Then he said to them, " My soul is overwhelmed with sorrow to the point of death. Stay here and keep watch with me." "

John 12 : 27.
" (27) " Now my soul is troubled, and what shall I say? ' Father, save me from this hour'? No, it was for this very reason I came to this hour." "

4.

(The Voice)

Job 7 : 11.
" (11) Like
Eliphaz , I will not
keep silent. In the

agony of my spirit, I
will speak; In the
bitterness of my
soul, I will
complain."

Job 10 : 1.
" (1) Job : I hate
my life, so i will
unload the full
weight of my
grievance against

God.
Let me speak and reveal the bitterness I am harboring."

Psalm 42 : 5 - 6.
" (5) Why am I so overwrought? Why am I so disturbed ?

Why can't I just hope in God?

Despite all my emotions, I will believe and praise the One who saves me and is my life.

(6) My God, my soul is so traumatized : the only help is remembering You

wherever I may
be;
From the land
of the Jordan to
Hermon's high
place
to Mount Mizar."

Psalm 42 : 11.

" (11) Why am
I so overwrought,
Why am I so
disturbed?
Why can't I
just hope in God?
Despite all
my emotions, I will
believe and praise
the One who saves
me, my God."

Psalm 84 : 2.

" (2) How I long to be there - my soul is spent, wanting, waiting to walk in the courts of the Eternal.

My whole being sings joyfully to the living God."

Psalm 104 : 35.

" (35) But may those who hate Him, who act against Him, disappear from the face of this beautiful planet.

As for the Eternal, call Him

good, my soul.
Praise the Eternal!"

Isaiah 26 : 9.
" (9) At night I long for You with all that is in Me.
When morning comes, I seek You with all my heart.

For when Your justice is done on earth, then everyone in the world will learn righteousness. "

Isaiah 38 : 15.
" (15) But what can I say? God has spoken to me. Things are as He

made them.

So I determined to go slowly, make the most of my years,

even though I am bitter to the core."

Isaiah 61 : 10.

" (10) I am filled with joy and my soul vibrates with exuberant hope, because of the Eternal my God;

For He has dressed me with the garment of salvation,

wrapped me with the robe of righteousness.

It's as though I'm dressed for my wedding day, in the very best: a bridegroom's garland and a bride's jewels."

Jeremiah 32 : 41.
" (41) It will be My great joy to do good things for them, and you can be sure that I will devote Myself completely to planting them anew in this land."

Micah 6 : 7.
" (7) Would
the Eternal be
pleased by
thousands of
sacrificial rams,
by ten
thousand swollen
rivers of sweet
olive oil?
Should I offer

my oldest son for my wrongdoing, the child of my body to cover the sins of my life? "

Matthew 11 : 29 - 30.

" (29) Put My yoke upon your shoulders - it might appear heavy at first, but it is perfectly fitted to your curves. Learn from Me, for I am gentle and humble of heart. When you are yoked to me, your weary souls will find rest.

(30) For My yoke is easy, and My burden is light."

Matthew 26: 37 - 38.

" (37) Then He took Peter and the two sons of Zebedee with Him, and He grew sorrowful and deeply distressed.

Jesus : (38) My soul is overwhelmed with grief, to the point of death. Stay here and keep watch with Me. "

John 12 : 27 - 28

" (27) My spirit is low and unsettled. How can I ask the Father to save me from this hour? This hour is the purpose for which I have come into the world. But what I can say is this :

(28) " Father, glorify Your name!..... ....." "

5.

(GNT)

Job 7 : 11.
" (11) No ! I
can't be quiet !
I am angry and

bitter.
I have to speak."

Job 10 : 1.
" (1) I am tired
of living.
Listen to my
bitter complaint."

Psalm 42 : 5 - 7.

"(5) Why am I
so sad ?
Why am I so
troubled?
I will put my
hope in God,
and once again
I will praise him.
my savior and
my God.
(6 -7) Here in

exile my heart is
breaking,
    and so I turn
my thoughts to
him.
    He has sent
waves of sorrow
over my soul;
    chaos roars at
me like a flood,
    like waterfalls

thundering down
to the Jordan
from Mount Hermon
and Mount Mizar."

Psalm 42 : 11.
" (11) Why am I
so sad?
Why am I so
troubled?
I will put my

hope in God,
  and once again I
will praise him,
  my savior and my
God."

  Psalm 84 : 2.
  " (2) How I want to
be there !
  I long to be in the
LORD'S Temple.

With my whole
being I sing for joy
to the living
God."

Psalm 104 : 35.
" (35) May sinners
be
destroyed from
the earth;

may the wicked
be no more.

Praise the LORD,
my soul!
Praise the LORD!"

Isaiah 26 : 9.
" (9) At night I
long for you
with all my
heart;

when you judge
the earth and its
people,
    they will all
learn what justice
is."

    Isaiah 38 : 15.
   " (15) What can
I say? The LORD
has done this.

My heart is bitter, and I cannot sleep."

Isaiah 61 : 10.
"(10) Jerusalem rejoices because of what the LORD has done.
She is like a bride dressed for her

wedding.
God has clothed her with salvation and victory."

Jeremiah 32 :41.
" (41) I will take pleasure in doing good things for them, and I will establish them

permanently in this land."

Micah 6 :7.

" (7) Will the LORD be pleased if I bring him thousands of sheep or endless streams of olive oil? Shall I offer him my first - born child to pay for my sins?"

117

Matthew 11 : 29 - 30.

" (29) Take my yoke and put it on you, and learn from me, because I am gentle and humble in spirit; and you will find rest.

(30) For the yoke I will give you is easy, and the load I will put on you is light."

Matthew 26 : 37 - 38.

" (37) He took with him Peter and the two sons of Zebedee. Grief and anguish came over him,

(38) and he said to them, " The sorrow in my heart is so great that it almost crushes me. Stay here and keep watch with me."

John 12 : 27 - 28.

" (27) " Now my heart is troubled - and what shall I say? Shall I say, ' Father, do not let this hour come upon me'? But that is why I came - so that I might go through this hour of suffering. (28) Father, bring glory to your name !" "

123

124

129

131

132

133

6.

Within this chapter we will give some consideration to the verses

from the
Book of Job.
We will seek
to view the
soul through
the very lens
of the verses
from Job?

Most people know very well the tale of the Man called Job and his life and times? In the times of the Old Testament , there was a division of the individual into

' body and soul and sometimes spirit?' There is a division made between ' body and soul ' in the various writings and the very books of the Old Testament. There was an inherent dichotomy made between the body and the soul?

137

In many ways, it is this dichotomy that is on show in the verses from the Book of Job that have been cited by this very book. Yet, one verse also talks about the spirit; Job 7 : 11 (ESV). Even given this, there seems to have been a sharp line drawn between a person having a body and a soul. The spirit of a person was something that the Lord God Almighty gave to a person or individual. The reality, is that, the terms of soul and spirit were used by

the writer's of the Old
Testament
interchangeably ...
one writer could refer
exclusively to the
spirit of a person and
another writer the
soul of a person.
In some ways,
it is made all the more
interesting by the
very reality of the

Hebraic view of a person as being a holistic individual. The individual parts had to be viewed in terms and in relation to the whole person. One part could tell us so much about the whole person and what they were like?

The simple reality, seen from the verses cited from the Book of Job, is that, one could talk objectively about how one's very soul was doing? Job's soul was generally downcast because what he was going through in his life .

In some ways, I wonder if that is a bad thing and may be well that we as people of our days and our times should be doing more of this talking to our souls. It would seem to me that we do not do enough of this sort of talking to our own soul's.

In Job 10 : 11 (ESV) we have the introduction of the very idea and notion of a person having a ' bitterness of the soul'? The simple reality, is that, we like Job the Man can often speak to both the Lord God Almighty, through the Son of God, Jesus Christ and our fellow human beings out of the very real and raw ' bitterness of our own souls.' The tale of the Man called Job comes from a time long past and yet it still can and does speak to us today?

I would be sure that we could all think of people we know who have this ' bitterness of their souls'? In some ways, and to a degree, it would seem to a lot more common in our days and in our generations. All of which is why so many people spend so much time having ' therapy'? One thing I do know without a shadow of doubt, any doubt at all, is that, if we do not deal effectively with our own ' bitterness of our souls'; it can do a lot of damage to us !

Not only do we damage to ourselves with our festering ' bitterness of the soul '. But we can also do a lot of damage to other people in our lives if we do not deal with it in an effective manner. As we all know it is other's who usually suffer the most from our own ' bitterness of the soul ?' Let me encourage you to deal with your own ' bitterness of the soul '; if you become aware of it in your lives.

It would be remiss of me , if I did not point out a way, the main way of dealing with our own ' bitterness of the soul'? In the end, it is simply through giving the Lord Jesus Christ the right gratitude, He is due for all he has done for us , as His follower's. Just take a moment and again stand at the very foot of the Cross of Calvary and simply marvel at the very real and raw price He paid for our very ...

salvation. When we become lost in wonder and very real and raw awe and wonder at what he went through for us all , we tend to lose our own ' bitterness of the soul.'

Also, in terms of our own ..

' bitterness of the soul'; I would believe that the Lord Jesus Christ can heal us of this as well, as He can heal us of any and all physical aliments? Give Him your own , very real and raw ' bitterness of the soul' and watch what He does with it !

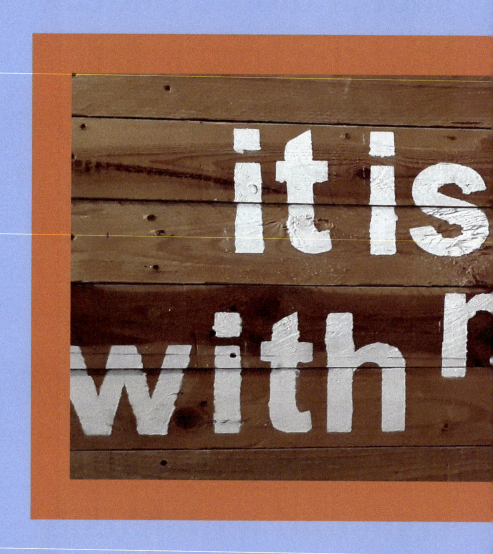

154

155

156

157

159

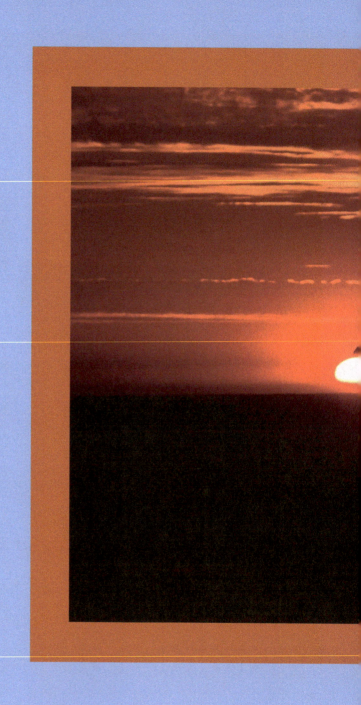

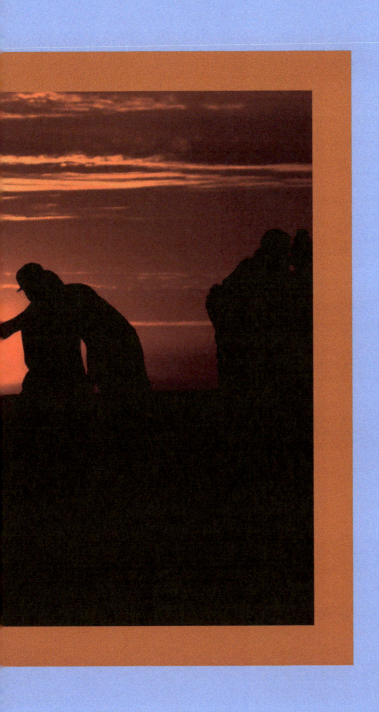

161

162

163

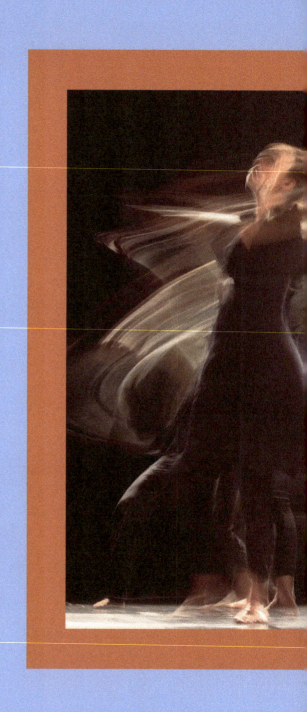

165

7.

In this chapter of the book, we will be giving some time to

considering the verses cited from the Psalter itself. It is from the Psalter that the title of this book .... comes?

It is in and through the very verses of the Psalter , that we get the very title of this book. As the Psalmist cried out : ' O My Soul, My Soul' so do we do too?

To myself this phrase is very much seen as a real and raw cry from the very heart and even soul of the person who pens these words in the Psalter. It is like they are crying out in very real and raw pain from the very depths of their heart and soul. May we be like them;

as we come before the Father through the Son of God, the Lord Jesus Christ in very real and raw repentance for all our wrongdoing's. It would seem to me that this is the sort of heart, mind and soul and even dare I say attitude of our whole

being that the Father
is looking for from us.
As we come before
Him, we need to and
should have this
attitude of heart,
mind and soul ....
...Laying it all on the
table of prayer before
Him ... Not holding
back anything ... Full
of emotion and pain !

As we saw from Job, some people can have a ' bitterness of the soul ?' I would believe that part of the very real antidote to this , is to cry out to the Father, the Lord God Almighty from the very depths of our heart's , mind's and even our soul's. Boldly approaching the throne of GRACE as we as follower's and believer's in the Lord Jesus Christ and His sacrifice upon the Cross of Calvary are able to do. It is when we adopt this very posture before the Father, the Lord God Almighty, that the very ' bitterness of the soul , our soul's ' can and will disappear and dissipate. That's of course , assuming we do want the ' bitterness of our soul's ' to be gone?

In some ways, I would see the cries from the very heart of the Psalmist as being very real and incredibly raw cries from their very heart's. It is like they have been able to capture in a few word's , some of the way and ways , we can all feel from time to time. I do not know about you but at times, I can find it hard to read the Psalter itself because of the very real and raw words contained in it's Psalms. It is like the Psalmist realizes that they cannot hope to hide anything from the Lord God Almighty and so they leave everything on the table? They pour out their innermost emotions and thoughts at any given point in time. All of which, is why it can be hard for one to read in our days?

In our days of so - called ' private Christianity' , one would wonder whether there is in reality the same heart and soul cries from the very people of the Lord God today? Or may well be , that in our days and in our generations we think we can hide and keep things from the Father, the Lord God Almighty? This may not be far removed from reality, in that, the evidence's for it would seem to come out of the way and ways we can be so guarded in our speech, even with the people of God.

Psalm 84 : 2 is worth talking about and noting in this very book. It has much to say to us, if we would only hear it? The very real and raw question for you and myself, is do we long with our very soul's to be in the very courts of the Father, the Lord God Almighty, through the Lord Jesus Christ. I must confess , there are times I do not want to be in His courts. May well be, that you feel like this at times , as the tides and times of the world - at - large flood into your own life?

All of which brings us to another point to note from Psalm 84 : 2. That is, that we can never be too far away from the very PRESENCE of the Father, the Lord God Almighty through His Son, the Lord Jesus Christ. At times, we may feel that He is distant and removed from ourselves and our life and it's situations. Yet, nothing could be further from the truth!

My own belief, as a follower of the Lord Jesus Christ, is that, once you have been saved , His very PRESENCE remains with you at all times, through the Holy Spirit's PRESENCE? For some, this is hard to accept and even affirm? They instead would rather believe that it is hit or miss; and that you can be too far away from and distant from the Lord Jesus Christ. This view would be supported by some of the Old Testament text's but it is a whole new and a very different ball - game after the times of the New Testament and the gifting by the Lord Jesus Christ of the Holy Spirit, who is the Lord God Himself? We are now, as it were carriers of the very PRESENCE of the Father, the Son of God

and the Holy Spirit.
We are now, carriers
of the very Presence
of the triune Godhead,
the trinity, the three -
persons in ONE LORD
GOD. Therefore, we
can never be too far
removed from the
very PRESENCE of the
Lord God Almighty.

Finally, in this chapter , we will seek to deal with Psalm 104 : 35 and it's contents and their meaning? In our days and in our generations one wonders how appropriate these words are? In some ways, these words have to be seen against the backdrop of the consuming passion the Psalmist had for the Lord God Almighty ... For him it was his burning passion ... He could not bear to think or believe that the sinners and those who did not know the Lord God Almighty would survive and even prosper. To a degree, I wonder whether or not we have the same or similar zeal for both the NAME and the RENOWN of the Lord God Almighty today?

In the end, we know the outcome is for people who do not accept and know the Lord Jesus Christ. All of which, should fuel our own witness to the Lord Jesus Christ. As we can understand both the immediacy and urgency of the times?

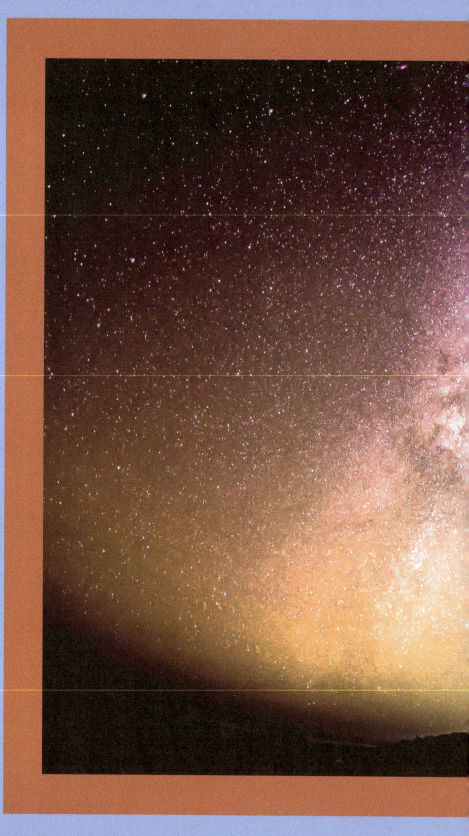

197

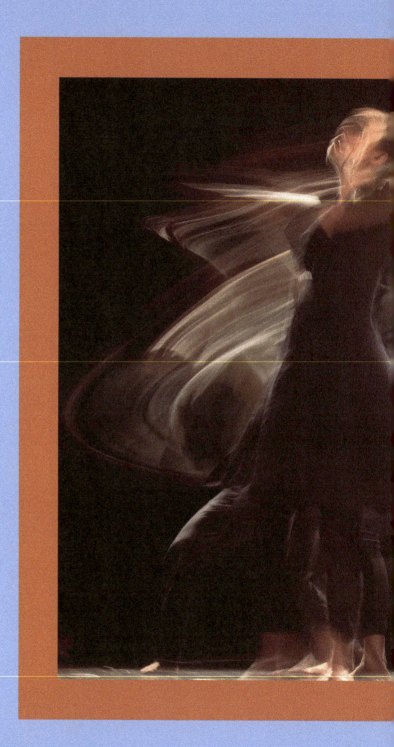

198

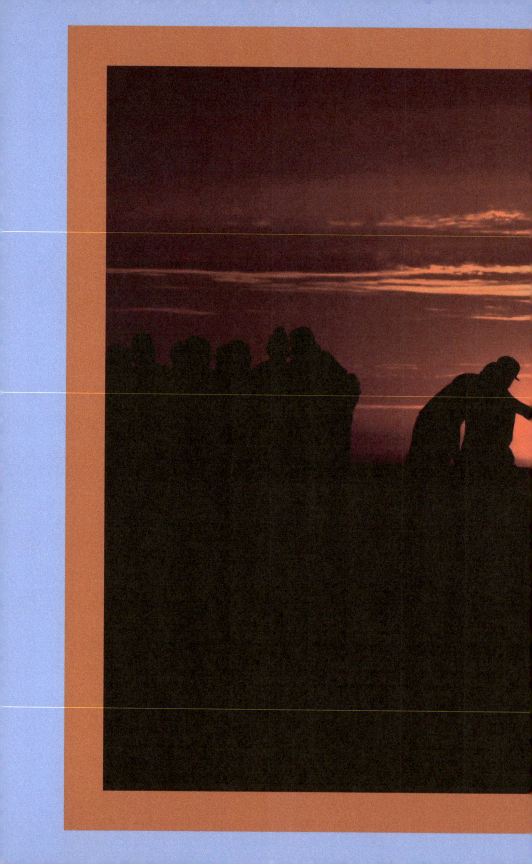

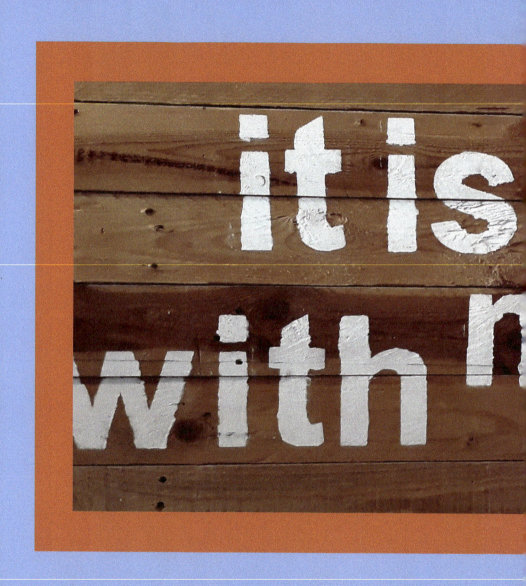

202

203

8.

We will now give some consideration to the rest of the Citations

from the Old Testament? Thinking about how they relate to the concept of the soul?

In the first Isaiah verse , we have the notion of the yearning of the soul for the Lord God Almighty; Isaiah 26 : 9. Again, as was noted to before, there is a real need for us to have a real yearning of our souls.

As in this verse , the yearning's of our soul's need to be for the Lord God Almighty. Our pursuit of the Father, the Lord God Almighty, through the very Son of God, the Lord Jesus Christ needs to be our yearning of the soul?

In the end, we do not have this yearning of our soul's for the Father, the Lord God Almighty? Or at least, speaking for myself, I do not always have this very yearning for the Father, the Lord God Almighty. I do not know about you ? It might well be , that you always have this very yearning's of the soul for the Father, the Lord God Almighty, through the very Son of God, the Lord Jesus Christ, always on tap? It is so easy to be fake about this. But let me encourage you to be very honest with yourself and other's on this matter of yearning's after the Father, yearning's of the soul for the Lord God Almighty.

The verse goes on to talk about this very yearning for the Father, the Lord God

Almighty, in relation to His judgment's of people upon the earth. All of which is a very different sort of yearning; or at least I tend to think so? The thing to remember , is that, the Father, the Lord God Almighty always judges righteously and with justice in all his judgment's upon the earth.

Therefore, it is interesting to note that the Father, the Lord God Almighty that the writer of Isaiah is thinking of and speaking about is the real one. He is not the Lord God Almighty, the Father, the ONE he has just imagined in his own mind's eye.... It is in reality, the Lord God Almighty, Father God , as seen in the very pages and writings of the Old Testament.

It is interesting that the notion of the ' bitterness of the soul ' comes up again in the verses from the Book of Isaiah. It occurs in Isaiah 38 : 15 ... which talks about ...

the ' bitterness of the soul '? In this verse, we are given a vision of the effects, some of the very real effects that a very real and raw ' bitterness of the soul ' can have upon an individual. Here we have the Prophet Isaiah himself being affected by a very real and raw ' soul bitterness '. This came out of the Prophecies he had to impart from the Lord God Almighty to King Hezekiah? Yet, in the end, it is still a very real and raw; ' soul bitterness?'

It might well the very real case in our times and in our days, when the Lord God Almighty gives you a so - called ' heavy' word or words of rebuke for a person or person's? This is the closest thing, to the situation of the Prophet Isaiah and what he was facing in those times, before the court of the King of Israel?

Yet, again we have the idea and notion of the very real and raw ' bitterness of the soul ' introduced again in the pages and verses of the Old

Testament. Through this verse in Isaiah 38 : 15 it is raised again for us , as reader's of the very pages of the Old Testament. However, the very real difference , is that, this time it is associated with the giving and proclamation of Prophecies from the

Lord God Almighty. In the end, it is still a ' bitterness of the soul' that is on show. It does develop, the very idea and notion of the whole thing of a ' bitterness of the soul'?

The final verse from Isaiah ; Isaiah

61 : 10 goes to the other extreme and talks about the soul exulting in the Lord God Almighty. In this very verse , the exultation of the soul and the Lord God Almighty is tied - in with what He has done for the person. It is caught up, very

much with the saving grace of the Lord God Almighty and the very act and acts of salvation that have taken place in a person's life.

The person's soul exults in the Lord God Almighty because He sees them as being righteous? It is because the Lord God Almighty has imparted His own righteousness to the person who is talking in the verse from Isaiah; Isaiah 61 : 10. All of which, is very interesting , in that, in our times , we too should be exulting in

the imputed
righteousness ; we
gain from the Lord
Jesus Christ. We gain
and get this through
His very death upon
the Cross of Calvary,
in our place. Because
of all of this we have
much more reason to
exult the Lord God
Almighty from within

our very soul's.

This very verse ,
is also interesting, in
that, it is how the
Lord God Almighty,
the Father sees a
person , an individual
who knows Himself.
The robe of
righteousness , echoes
very much the work

of the Lord Jesus Christ as the ' perfect sacrifice ' upon the very Cross of Calvary. We as believer's and follower's of the Lord Jesus Christ are seen by His Father and our Father, the Lord God Almighty dressed in a robe of righteousness. The one that was ...

paid for and bought for us by the work of the Lord Jesus Christ upon the very Cross of Calvary.

The verse from Jeremiah, is also highly relevant to our ongoing discussion of the soul; that is, Jeremiah 32 : 41. One has to think of this verse , in terms of humanity being made in the very ' imago deo '; that is, the image of God. From it we gain the notion that the Lord God Almighty has a heart and a soul? It would seem in some way and ways, the writer is talking about the Lord God Almighty in human terms, terms that we can identify with..... The question is does the Lord God Almighty, really have a heart and a soul? All of which, is very interesting to think about , given that humanity is in fact ....

made in the image of God, the ' imago deo'? In the end, one does not want to push the imagery associated with this too far and too extremes ... The Father, the Lord God Almighty , is still the Lord God; unlike us in so many ways. He is Spirit , for starter's ;

we are spirit as well but His being is Spirit? Therefore, in the end , the imagery and the very ramifications of humanity being made in the image of the Lord God , the ' imago deo' can be pushed too far at times and in this case it will not be taken to extremes.

The final Old Testament verse to be considered by this book , is Micah 6 : 7? It is a very interesting verse, in that, it introduces the notion of the soul sinning and doing the wrong thing. Therefore, from this very verse we are left with the notion that the soul can in reality and in fact be sinful and do the wrong thing. In the end, I would believe that is the whole person that is sinful and does the wrong thing? I say this, because of the holistic nature of Hebraic thought ... one part of a person represented the whole of the person and individual. The point, is that, it may well allude to the reality and the fact of the soul of a man being sinful and doing the wrong thing. But in the end, I would believe it is just representative of the whole person and their own standing as an individual before the Lord God Almighty, the Father, the Son of God and the Holy Spirit?

238

239

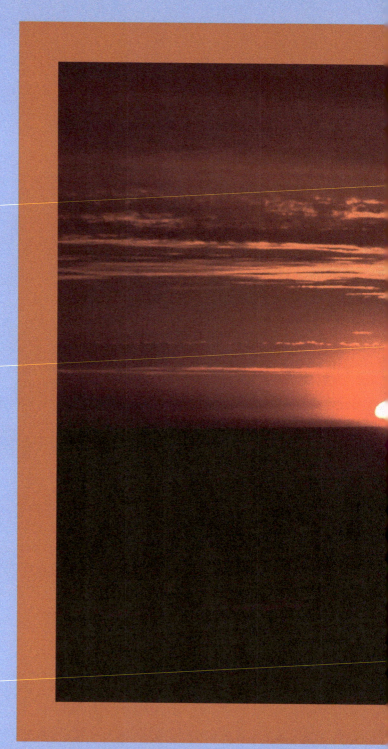

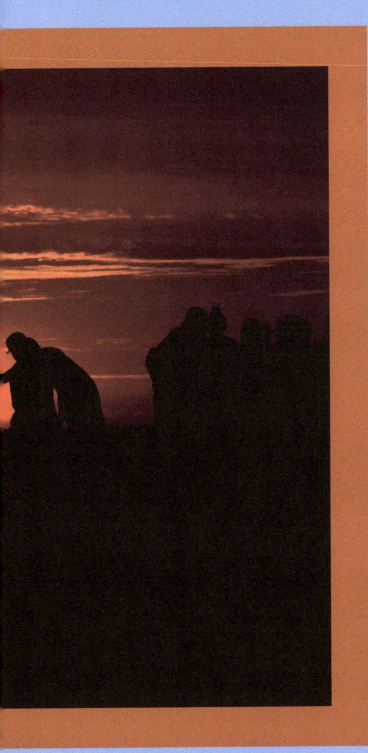

244

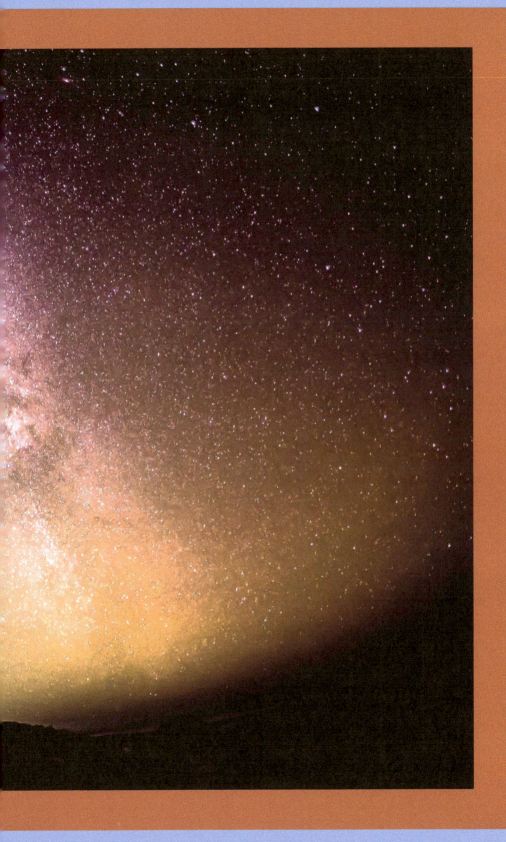

9.

Let us now give some consideration to Matthew

11 : 29 - 30
and come to have a look at what it has to say regarding the soul?

In Matthew 11 : 29 - 30 , we have the idea of finding ' rest ' for our very souls introduced. We can have rest for our very souls in the taking up of the very yoke of the Lord Jesus Christ?

In some ways, there is a conflict in the imagery of the yoke and finding rest in the very yoke of the Lord Jesus Christ. We would rightly think to be yoked to someone or something is to be not at rest. Further we would commonly think and believe that to be yoked is to be oppressed and even restrained oppressively? Yet, in this verse , the Lord Jesus Christ is in fact saying that it is when we are yoked to Him that we find real rest for our very souls. In some ways, we have lost the imagery that the Lord Jesus Christ was using at this time. We all do not live on farms and around animals, in our days. However, if we can get the imagery, then we can get a profound message from the Lord Jesus Christ about what it is like to be found in Him and through Him.

The other idea to take away from these verses in Matthew , is that, it is very apparent that the soul itself can be not at peace. We would not find rest in the yoke of the Lord Jesus Christ if our souls were always at peace in themselves. Therefore, the very real implication of the verse , is simply that , we find real

and lasting peace
from the very turmoil
within our very souls.
The turmoil comes
from the various
warring factions,
drives and even
desires that war
within our very souls.
A key to seeing this,
is when the Lord
Jesus Christ talks ...

about how he is gentle, lowly and humble in heart. It is in knowing and following the Lord Jesus Christ in our very lives that we can find the very rest He is talking about here for our very souls.

The aspect of the soul to gain from

Matthew 11 : 29 - 30 is simply that, at times our very souls within can be and are usually in very real turmoil without the yoke of the Lord Jesus Christ. It is when we are in relationship with Him and become follower's of Him , that we can and do find very real rest and peace for our very souls. Again, we need at this point to remember that the soul is the whole person, so therefore; the whole person finds rest and peace when they are yoked to the Lord Jesus Christ!

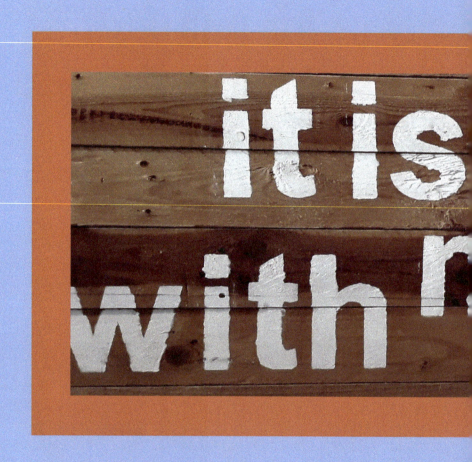

260

263

264

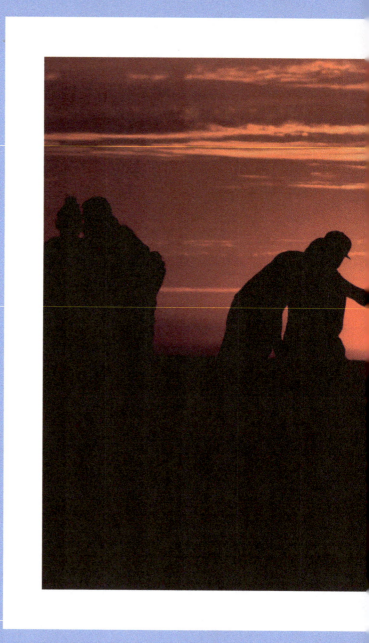

266

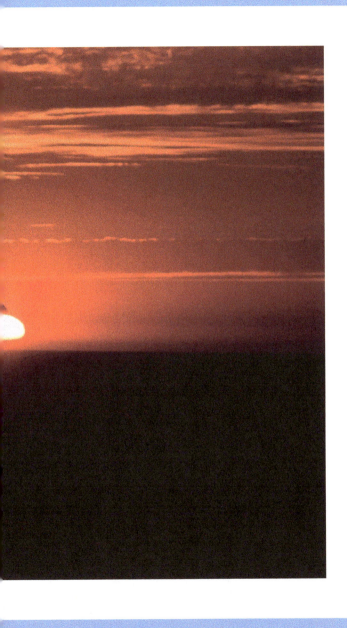

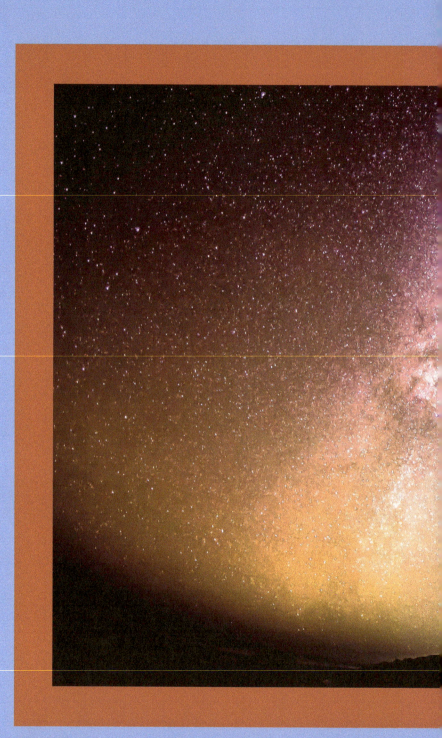

10.

Now let us give some time to the last two verses cited.

They are : Matthew 26 : 37 - 38 and John 12 : 27 - 28. They are as follows : (ESV) Matthew 26 : 37 - 38.

" (37) And taking with him Peter and the two sons of Zebedee , he began to be sorrowful and troubled.

(38) Then he said to them, " My soul is very sorrowful, even to death; remain here, and watch

with me."

(ESV) John 12 : 27 - 28 " (27)" Now is my soul troubled. And what shall I say?

' Father, save me from this hour'? But for this purpose I have come to this hour. (28) ' Father, glorify your name.' "

These verses
are in many ways ,
the punch - line of
this very book; ' O
My Soul, My Soul'?
In many, so many
ways, this is what
the book has been
leading up to. May

we take them
seriously and come
to a very real
understanding and
acceptance of them.

The verses
are situated in the
hours before the
Lord Jesus Christ
was arrested in the
Garden. He is both

speaking them out aloud and I would believe at the same time praying them to His Father in Heaven ..... They are very real and very raw in their emotional content; words offered by the Lord Jesus at this very point in time. He knows He is about to face death upon the very Cross of Calvary and His soul is much troubled .... Therefore , one's soul can be very troubled ... even as the ONE who was and is the Messiah, the ONE who would die upon the Cross of Calvary for all Humanity...

The point, is simply that, if the ONE who flung stars into space soul can be troubled, our soul's can be troubled as well? Given further, if we are in reality made in the ' imago deo'; the very Image of God, then we too . like the Lord Jesus Christ, just before He went to the Cross can have troubled soul's. I will admit however, we do not face in anyway what He was facing in terms of the Cross of Calvary. Yet, my point is simply that, we too can have troubled soul's? Furthermore, He was and is the God

Man; He was and is like one of us, human beings and yet, fully God at the same time. All of which is a mystery in itself? The reality , is that, He was like us and He had a troubled soul in this instance. My reason

for mentioning this
at this juncture, is
simply because at
times we can all
feel it is somehow
wrong to be
troubled and at
unease within our
very soul's. If the
Lord Jesus Christ
could be troubled in
his very soul, then
286

it is alright for us to troubled in our very soul's as well?

There are some who would say that a follower of the Lord Jesus Christ should never ever be sorrowful or troubled in their very soul. I would believe that these very verses from Matthew's and John's Gospels deal effectively with this belief. There are times and even places it is alright for a follower of the Lord Jesus Christ to be both sorrowful and even dare I say, troubled in their very soul. A case in point would be when somebody who is close to us, a family member dies, we grieve and can feel very real and raw sorrow about their death?

In conclusion; I want us to think through whether or not the Lord Jesus Christ had any real ' bitterness of the soul'? Mainly because as one reads these verses one could arrive at this conclusion without too much effort and strain mentally and intellectually. Throughout this book, one of the things we have been thinking about is ' bitterness of the soul '. We have seen how the man called Job had it , as well as the Prophet Isaiah. So, the question before us is, ' did the Lord Jesus Christ have any at all, that is, ' bitterness of His soul ' as He went to the Cross ? The short and very simple answer to this very question, is that, He did not have any ' bitterness of His soul'. I say this, in that, as the text itself states , His soul was troubled and not bitter and having any form of

' bitterness of the soul ' in it.

We may at times have a very real ' bitterness of the soul ' and yet, in this instance of the life and times of the Lord Jesus Christ I do not know that He had any? Admittedly; His very soul was troubled but the very texts do not give any inkling of any real and raw ' bitterness of the soul ' on His part. All of which, is part and parcel of what makes the Lord Jesus Christ truly the Messiah !

There are two points finally, one is that,the Lord Jesus Christ did not have any form of ' bitterness of the soul ' as He faced the Cross of Calvary. Also, that it is alright , and natural for us as

His follower's to at times have souls that are in reality troubled and at unease within themselves. On this point, I want you all to understand it is alright to be at times troubled in your own soul?

11.

EPILOGUE :

How does one even begin to sum up this ...

304

book? It is always the problem I face as I finish and wrap up a book.

In the end,

a question I have for all of you; ' is it well with your soul?' Your answer to this question is one you have to be honest with yourself about. It is also a question that you alone can answer for yourself?

In this book, we have seen how it is at times possible for one to have a ' bitterness of the soul?' In relation to this, think of the very real and raw examples of both Job and the Prophet Isaiah from the

Old Testament. Both of these men had a very real and very raw in emotion's ' bitterness of their soul's'? The thing to take away from both examples , is that, it is alright to have one in yourself as well. Further, we saw from the New Testament citations , how the Lord Jesus Christ can be the ...

ONE who is both the answer and also the ONE who can give our very soul's rest in Him !

In conclusion, we also looked at how the Lord Jesus Christ was troubled in His soul . Yet , He did not have any real and raw ' bitterness of His soul' before He went to the very Cross . Both which should

and do speak
to us , as His
follower's in our
days and in our
generations.
After the Cross
of Calvary and

all that happened upon it and through it in our very lives today. The Lord Jesus

Christ was one of us, a human being fully and yet he had no ' bitterness of His soul '. As He went to the

Cross of Calvary to die a death, as an innocent man for all of humanity and their forgiveness by the Father!

320

321

12.

THE
AUTHOR:

JOHN C BURT

323

JOHN WORSHIPS AT ST. PHILLIPS , ANGLICAN CHURCH, AUBURN, NSW, AUSTRALIA.

JOHN LOVES COFFEE, PIZZA AND CHICKEN AND JELLYFISH , IN THAT ORDER, AS LONG AS THE COFFEE IS HOT!

AMEN.

and

AMEN!

SHALOM

DEAR LORD JESUS, MAY WE FIND REST FOR OUR VERY SOULS IN KNOWING, BELIEVING IN AND FOLLOWING YOU!

AMEN....

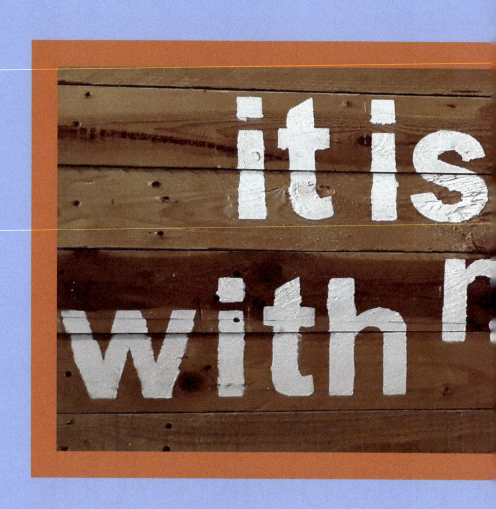

329

332

333

CPSIA information can be obtained
at www.ICGtesting.com
Printed in the USA
LVHW011703090320
649440LV00008B/211